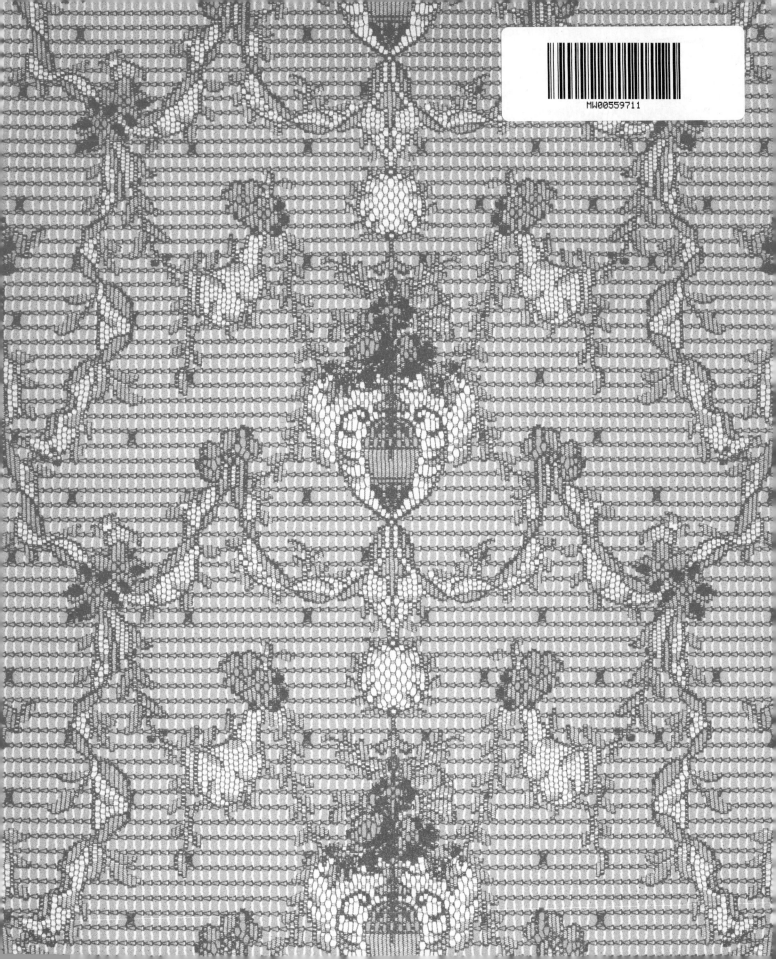

FADED GLAMOUR

FADED GLAMOUR

inspirational interiors and beautiful homes

PEARL LOWE

ART DIRECTION BY RACHEL ASHWELL

PHOTOGRAPHY BY AMY NEUNSINGER

CICO BOOKS

LONDON NEW YORK

This book is dedicated to my Dad, who I miss every single day. May he rest in peace.

Published in 2019 by CICO Books
An imprint of Ryland Peters & Small Ltd
20–21 Jockey's Fields   341 E 116th St
London WC1R 4BW   New York, NY 10029

www.rylandpeters.com

10 9 8 7 6 5 4 3 2

A CIP catalog record for this book is available from the Library of Congress and the British Library.

ISBN: 978 1 78249 791 2

Printed in China

Designer: Geoff Borin
Photographer: Amy Neunsinger
Art director: Rachel Ashwell
Words by: Natasha Garnett
Endpapers: Morton, Young & Borland Textiles

Editor: Anna Galkina
In-house art director: Sally Powell
Head of production: Patricia Harrington
Publishing manager: Penny Craig
Publisher: Cindy Richards

Contents

introduction

Since an early age I have been attracted to all things vintage – from the clothes I wear and base my own designs on, to the curios I'm drawn to, magpie-like, when visiting an antiques fair or a junk shop. I love the decadence of the 1920s: show me a lampshade with a tasselled fringe and I have to have it. I'm constantly entranced by the sheer glamour of a rococo piece – no matter how chipped it may be when it inevitably crosses my threshold. Old bevelled mirrors and the twinkle of a chandelier or candelabra bring the right kind of light into my life. When it comes to textiles, silks and velvets add a sense of sophistication regardless of how worn or faded they may be. Carpets and rugs give colour and warmth, even if a little threadbare. Chintz takes me back in time and animal prints make me smile. But, if I had to pick one textile above all others, then it would have to be vintage lace. Indeed, such is my passion for lace that my first venture into the world of interiors began when I started making lace curtains for my friends on my kitchen table in London twenty years ago. A piece of lace, no matter how small, conjures up a sense of history and sheer romanticism – and as I discovered back then, when hand-dyed hot pink or electric blue it takes on a whole new lease on life.

How to define *Faded Glamour*? Well, to sum it up, I'd say it's a gloriously decadent yet well-lived-in decorating style. I think of rooms that are elegant yet whimsical at the same time. Precious pieces of antique furniture that have become slightly battered over decades while holding their allure become all the more charming when playfully juxtaposed with a more contemporary, colourful piece from a flea market. It's the point where eighteenth-century mahogany wood meets 1950s plastic retro; where chintz sits alongside animal print and sultry velvets; rococo suddenly goes a little rock 'n' roll; and a freestanding 1970s Anglepoise lamp sets it all alight. Rooms that are opulent and grand, yet loved-and-lived-in; houses with a story to tell beneath their patina. That, to me, is very much the essence

RIGHT Sera Hersham Loftus' dressing room, lined with antique French shutters as an alternative to wardrobe doors. Her collection of ballet shoes hangs from the doors.

LEFT A view of Marianne Cotterill's bathroom, embellished with a beautiful iridescent crystal chandelier.

of faded glamour – it's a style I absolutely adore and have adopted over the years in my own houses and when decorating those of my clients.

I suppose many people might regard my style as quite 'eclectic', and even if they don't mean that as a wholehearted compliment, that's fine by me because I don't believe there should be any rules – unless you want your house to look like a hotel. It's about the mix, the alchemy you create when you play around with styles. Yes, I want to live in an environment that is aesthetically beautiful and artistic, but where I live is also my home and I want it to look and feel like that. I don't want to have rooms that are unused; a dining room that only sees the light of day at Christmas or a drawing room that's out of bounds to children and pets.

My inspiration comes from so many quarters – art, film, photography, music, work, travel and above all, my friends, and I'd have say one of the greatest influencers in honing my own sense style would have to be Rachel Ashwell, the designer and writer who, in the nineties, introduced us all to 'shabby chic', a style that her name has become synonymous with. What her work and her eye have taught me was how to create living spaces that are not just decadent and stylish, but deliciously inviting and alluringly comfortable.

In the pages that follow, as well as looking at my own home, I'm also going to walk you through the homes of some friends of mine that I think have nailed the faded glamour look – in all its glory and different incarnations. I'm going to take you into the property of one of the most renowned names in British fashion, whose historic house has gone a bit disco; a designer who, famous for the clean lines of his stunning contemporary furniture, has adorned his rural retreat with stunning antiques; a jewellery designer who set her cottage alight in a blaze of gemstone colours. I'll even introduce you to an acclaimed Paris-based fashion interiors guru, who has not only transformed a derelict farmhouse into an achingly hip art hub, but in the process has, somehow, managed to make avocado bathrooms cool again.

Everyone included here, friends from London and Somerset – all great creatives – has their own unique interpretation of faded glamour, but as different as each house is, I can honestly say there isn't one that I wouldn't happily call my home.

My Faded Glamour

LEFT When I first decorated the dining room with a pale grey wallpaper I realised instantly I'd made a mistake – it was austere and not 'us', so I redecorated it with Midnight Garden wallpaper from House of Hackney that I had been lusting after for years and what was once an uninviting room has been brought to life.

OVERLEAF In the drawing room, I wanted to create a sense of country-house grandeur, but at the same time I wanted this room to be used all the time, not only when we were entertaining. Vast sofas – a red velvet from Rachel Ashwell and one reupholstered in fabric from Nicholas Herbert – put together with leather club chairs and a tiger-print Ottoman make this the ideal room for relaxing, while the antique mirror and my collection of rococo furniture give it a sense of elegance.

When I first set eyes on the Georgian property we live in today, my heart sang, as I knew I had found the house of my dreams. Built in the 1820s of warm yellow Bath stone – which takes on a dreamy golden hue at sunset – it has curved walls and arched windows and its walled garden is simply magical. Classic in design yet manifold with architectural quirks. It spoke to my sense of style, and that was even before I walked through the door – the search for my perfect home was finally over.

I stress the word 'finally' here because, from the moment my husband Danny Goffey and I decided to uproot from London and move our family to the country fifteen years ago, our quest to find the perfect house had been epic, to say the least, and in the intervening years we moved at least six times.

You see, as determined as we were to make the leap from the city to the country – primarily to give our children a rural upbringing – when we put our lovely stucco house in the heart of London's Camden on the market, I don't think either of us had ever really considered what our bucolic dream would look like in real life. Suffice it to say, we had a naïve fantasy of what it would be – all rose-covered porches, woods filled with bluebells, babbling brooks and log fires – but we hadn't really considered the practicalities.

Our first house, for example, was in easy reach of London. That seemed ideal on paper, but what we hadn't factored in was that living in a commuter town meant we were surrounded by weekenders – great on a Saturday night, but in the week we might as well have been living in a ghost town. In moving west to Somerset, with its beauty and a community of like-minded friends, we seemed to have found our spiritual home, but still, mistakes were made.

We first lived in the middle of a town that I adore, but there simply wasn't enough outdoor space for the children; we then perched ourselves on top of

LEFT In the corner of the dining room is an antique wedding dome – which was a birthday gift from Danny – from one of my favourite shops, Susannah in Bath.

RIGHT An old pink sink chair we bought from the Shepton Flea Market. It's a bit battered but I can't bring myself to recover it as I love the pink.

a hill surrounded by woodland – fairytale, but isolated. We upsized to a truly beautiful old rectory, only to realise that we were spending too many hours of each day in our cars ferrying the children around the county to their various schools and extracurricular activities. Yes, we were spending quality time here in the country as a family, but only on the road, not at home.

And then, just as we'd given up hope, we found this – a house of generous proportions; an abundance of character; with just enough garden to run wild in; one that was in the right location; the perfect house for all of us: me, Danny, our youngest Betty, sons Alfie and Frank and daughter Daisy.

ABOVE, LEFT AND RIGHT
The woodwork in the dining room is painted in Farrow & Ball's Pitch Black. The oval table was made to fit the curve of the bay window. A tongue-and-groove window seat is cushioned in pink velvet and I painted the French café chairs to go with the colour scheme.

I've mentioned our moves here because despite all of those houses being so different, in each my style hasn't really changed. You could have walked into any of those properties and you'd have seen my signature pieces and touches – 1920s fringed lamps; rococo furniture; velvet; animal prints; piano shawls; lace tablecloths and curtains; and the colours intrinsic to my sense of decorative style, one that is described as bohemian, eclectic and rock 'n' roll romantic. But here, I've found the perfect backdrop where this can all be showcased fully. It's a house where my vision of faded glamour really works. Maybe that has something to do with the layout of the house – its generous

hallway, passageways, rambling staircases and interconnecting rooms and Georgian windows that allow the light in – made all the more beautiful with billowing curtains of silk, panels of lace, or dressed in swathes of velvet or sequins. On the ground and first floors, ceilings are high enough to allow for tall armoires, my collection of vintage chandeliers and for four-poster beds. There are also voluptuously rounded reception rooms, the perfect stage set in which to create a salon.

Beautiful as the house is, when we first took it on three years ago, Danny and I knew that this was going to be a project. Before I could even begin

LEFT A battered 1930s leather club chair bursting from the seams may have seen better days, but it is incredibly comfortable. I think a little wear-and-tear gives character to a piece of furniture and is so much more desirable than something new. It's softened here by a purple velvet cushion from Sera of London.

RIGHT The table in the hallway is by Eero Saarinen and I've dressed it with one of my 1920s piano shawls, which I have been collecting for years.

to think of decorating, structural work had to be done, from the stonework to the floors – where boards didn't just creak underfoot, they nearly collapsed. The kitchen not only had to be replaced, but moved to another room and bathrooms dealt with. All of these essentials had to be completed before we even thought about how to tackle the house's eleven bedrooms.

It is a large house, yes, but that's what we needed. Both Danny and I work from home, and I needed a workroom for my dress designs and my collection of children's clothes, as well as my interiors projects. And Danny, a musician and drummer with the band Supergrass, needed space to make music.

LEFT AND RIGHT Zebra and rococo sofas give the family a place to sit while Danny's cooking. On the kitchen wall is our collection of art, which includes the 'I'm Not Sorry' artwork from my best friend Zoe Grace, the lips print from the Swedish artist Bxxlght and a wonderful balloon print from our friend Sam Taylor-Johnson, which hangs over the AGA on the opposite side of the room.

OVERLEAF I approached deVOL to design a kitchen with me after Danny, the primary cook in the household, finally put his foot down and said we needed a proper 'working' one. The main part of the kitchen is made up of Shaker cupboards with a long marble worktop that gives Danny the space he needs.

As for the eleven bedrooms: with a large family they are a must, as even though the eldest children have essentially flown the nest, I always want them to have a room of their own when they are home, and on high days and holidays the house is usually full to the brim with our nearest and dearest.

With the structural work complete, the next step was to put my stamp on the house, which, while celebrating the heritage of this period property, paid homage to my own, more playful style.

In the drawing room, for example, I used a classic Robert Kime wallpaper, which would look perfect in any English country house of this era and it's set

LEFT The breakfast room, which leads directly off the kitchen, is where we eat when we don't have guests. The ceiling lamp came from the designer Lorraine Kirk, the chairs and cushions from a local antiques shop in Wells and the lace tablecloth was found in a flea market in Amsterdam.

RIGHT The black cupboards with glass windows in the island were specially designed for me by deVOL, as they didn't have any in their range. The metal bar stools are from Old Albion in Bridport. The floor is made of old elm boards I found in a reclamation yard – they cover the entire ground floor.

off by the wood and shutters which are painted in a dark black paint by Little Green. Large, groaning sofas – a red velvet from Rachel Ashwell and a chintzy, floral-upholstered one by Nicholas Herbert – and an antique mirror over the mantelpiece give the room that traditional feeling, but the addition of the tiger-print ottoman, a pair of slightly battered 1930s leather chairs, rococo side tables and 1920s fringed lamps suddenly gives the space a more salon-like feeling, especially when filled with people. It has a sense of grandeur and opulence but is also cosy enough for Danny and I to retreat to at night when

PREVIOUS PAGES As well as being havens of comfort, I always think bedrooms should feel luxurious and have a hint of glamour. My bed from Soho Home combines all of that, and the scalloped headboard gives it that injection of boudoir chic I so love. I've decorated the room in a palette of pale pinks and greens, one of my favourite colour combinations, to give the room a sense of tranquillity. The Keith Richards photograph by Derek Ridgers was a birthday gift from the music mogul Alan McGee.

LEFT My B & T Antiques dressing table has travelled with me from house to house over the years. The wallpaper is from Robert Kime, and I made the curtains from Kate Forman fabric – lined with blankets to keep the light and cold out.

RIGHT We inserted an armoire into a gap between the fitted wardrobes and then spray-painted the panelling.

we are on our own – lighting the fire before sinking into one of the sofas to read or watch old movies.

I wanted the salon-like feeling to flow through into the dining room, which is often a dead room in most houses because of the way we tend to live in open-plan kitchens. I wanted this room to be used and I was determined to make it as alluring as possible. By wallpapering it in a loud floral from House of Hackney, called Midnight Garden, and painting the woodwork the deepest of blacks, my aim was to create a room that was sultry and intimate when lit by candlelight and dressed with vases filled with blossoms from the garden.

PREVIOUS PAGES It took
many attempts to get our
bathroom right, but I think
we've finally got there with this
copper bath and Bert & May
zigzag tiles. The mirror above
the bath is from Lorraine Kirk.

LEFT, RIGHT AND
OVERLEAF The main spare
bedroom has been lined with
another wallpaper from Robert
Kime and I bought the bed
online from La Belle Étoffe –
I've dressed it here with a lace
bedspread I found on a trip to
Bath, a fur throw by Helen
Moore and velvet cushions from
Sera of London. To add to the
opulent feel of this guest room,
I've added an assortment of
rococo furniture and a beautiful
1920s screen, which I bought
from one of my favourite
treasure troves, Lark Vintage, in
Frome. The windows have been
dressed with lace from my
own collection.

Unable to find a table large enough for all our guests and the perfect shape to fill the curved bay of the window, I commissioned my long-suffering carpenter, Steve, to make one for us. It is covered in velvet zebra-print, which I decorated with a heavy tasseled fringe from V V Rouleaux. After filling the room with curios, what was once quite a challenging and cold room now has an ambience that is heady and inviting.

The kitchen was our one great expense, and as we love to entertain and knew this would be a room where we would spend the majority of our time, I have no regrets. Originally, this had been the dining room, but I swapped

PREVIOUS PAGES When it came to the design of my eldest daughter Daisy's bedroom and bathroom I wanted to create rooms that were serene yet had a bit of old Hollywood glamour. In the bathroom, we went to town with Lotus wallpaper from Farrow & Ball, mirrored tiles, a leopard-print button chair, a gilt mirror from Shepton Flea Market and a black-and-white print of Audrey Hepburn. Also in the room is my collection of religious figurines.

LEFT I originally bought the bed for a client, but when they didn't have room for it I knew that it was perfect for Daisy's room. The vintage butterfly mirror above the bed, bought from French General Trading in Frome, made me smile and I knew she would love it.

RIGHT A detail of a peacock on a 1920s silk screen I bought from Jane Bourvis on Portobello Road in London.

those rooms simply because here – thanks to the large French windows that open straight onto the lawn – there was more light and it had a better aspect.

To be honest, I've always had an aversion to fitted kitchens, preferring an assortment of reclaimed cupboards and armoires instead, but Danny, a consummate chef and the primary cook in our household, had one caveat when we moved here: to have a proper, functional kitchen – one where he didn't knock his head on a cupboard door constantly, the handles didn't fall off drawers, the sink drained without the use of a plunger and the oven didn't fail in the middle of a soufflé.

So I turned to deVOL to design a kitchen that would satisfy his culinary needs and my aesthetic. It has a long island, made up of Shaker cupboards with a marble top, which gives Danny the workspace he needs and room for all of us without getting under each other's feet. Originally, I'd planned for the kitchen to have an industrial look, but once it was in place, I decided it needed softening up – so antique pendant lights hang from the ceiling and our art collection lines the walls to add colour and personality – and it's now one of my favourite rooms in the house. A small, light breakfast room, leading off the main kitchen area and furnished with French farmhouse-style finds, is where we gather to eat when we are *en famille*.

As someone who values her sleep, I've always believed that bedrooms must be warm, inviting, and above all, comfortable. Although I try and eschew most things new, I will bend that rule when it comes to bedlinen, for as much as I like to indulge in that vintage look, when it comes to getting a good night's sleep, I need some twenty-first-century luxury. My own bed comes from Soho Home, which gives me the comfort I need, while the shell-like velvet headboard nods to a bygone era, and elsewhere in the house new memory foam mattresses are married with old bedframes and antique headboards, ensuring shut-eye, without compromising on style.

Aside from comfort, I believe that bedrooms – and bathrooms – should always feel luxurious. I love a bit of boudoir glamour when turning in for the night, and in our master bedroom I think I've achieved that. A palette of soft pinks and greens (one of my favourite colour combinations), a small-print Nicholas Herbert wallpaper, fringed glass lamps – which have been with me throughout the years – and a mirrored dressing table give this room a serene and feminine touch. A line of dated fitted wardrobes was given something of a French revival when we panelled them, inserted an armoire into a gaping hole between the set and Danny spray-painted the detailing, adding a touch of gold. Our bathroom – with its Bert & May zigzag tiles and freestanding copper bath – complements the bedroom, while being fabulously idiosyncratic at the same time.

With the main spare bedrooms and bathrooms, I've followed the lead of combining comfort and colour to create rooms with character. The Rust Room, as it has come to be known, is decorated in hues of orange and blue – which was never intentional but turned out to be a happy mistake – it's cosy,

LEFT I've been collecting vintage children's dress-up pieces for years – circus costumes, tutus and jester coats. Primarily, these were for the children as they always wanted to dress up, but sadly they have long grown out of that. I've hung on to them because they've been a useful archive when I've worked on my collections of children's clothing – and also because I love them!

RIGHT In my son Frank's bathroom, I decided to jazz up the rolltop bath by covering it in shocking pink velvet, which took quite a bit of patience and quite a lot of glue! The tiles on the floor come from Fired Earth.

OVERLEAF, LEFT A silk tassel livens up an old hand-painted cupboard.

OVERLEAF, RIGHT In Alfie's bedroom, we have used Lower George St. Beryl wallpaper by Little Green to line the room.

yet theatrical, thanks to a beautiful vintage screen. In another bedroom, a four-poster bed draped in vintage lace takes centre stage to create a whimsically romantic room. To inject a touch of old-Hollywood glamour, a tired old bathroom was wallpapered in Lotus from Farrow & Ball, the original panelling painted in dark oak and tiled with squares of antique mirrors.

Towards the top of the house, I adopted a more relaxed, countrified look to transform what had been a warren of cold, neglected rooms. By mixing up contrasting wallpapers – delicate vintage prints with bolder ones by William Morris, for example – I decided to make a feature out of the slanting ceilings.

LEFT The wallpaper used in this spare room is from Sister Parish and I bought the antique beds at auction. The purple velvet bedspread is another great find from Rachel Ashwell and the floral oil painting came from Shepton Flea Market.

RIGHT The stairs leading up from the ground floor to our room have been covered in a bright stripe runner from Roger Oates, called Kyoto Blossom.

Then, I filled every room with a mix of antique furniture and vibrantly painted junk-shop finds, colourful blankets, eiderdowns and throws. My aim was to create a cosy level of eclectic rooms to nestle into at night.

One other extravagance when redecorating this house has been wallpaper – Danny has recently been threatening to send me on a papering course so he can send me up a ladder to save on cost should, god forbid, we ever have to move again. But, wallpaper is a passion of mine (so much so, I recently launched my own line) and I believe that if you choose well then it should last the distance, and besides, I like it when it's a bit worn and faded over time.

LEFT AND RIGHT Upstairs in the attic are two further bedrooms. The first is wallpapered with a mixture of prints from Cole & Son (on the walls) and Lower George St. Beryl (on the ceiling). A pink velvet bed I bought in Brighton and a brightly-coloured rug I haggled for on my last trip to Marrakesh add warmth and colour to what was quite a dark room. The chair in front of the bed I found at the Holland Park boutique The Cross and the battered, pink velvet one I've had with me for years.

OVERLEAF In the second bedroom, I've used a paper by William Morris called Acanthus. The green and gold Rococo bedside table came from a flea market and Danny found the green dresser in La Belle Brocante, in Wells.

But where I have spent I have also saved. Fitted carpets, for example, are, for me, a false economy – unless you are enlivening a staircase with a runner – and especially if you live as we do. They would have to be replaced every couple of years with our muddy country foot – and paw – fall. You can't pass a fitted carpet onto your children, but you can pass on a beautiful old rug. Similarly, when it comes to fabrics, I always say to choose ones that you will want to live with for the rest of your life, because, as I have learned over the years, no matter how many times you move or your tastes change, they can always, with a nip and a tuck, be successfully reincarnated.

LEFT A view into Alfie's room from the William Morris spare room. The chandelier was bought from Lark Vintage in Frome.

RIGHT The fringed lamp was a purchase from Newbury Antiques & Collectors Fair, and the wonderfully ornate bedside table was another find from Shepton Flea Market.

There's an old adage I like to live by: 'one man's tat is another man's treasure.' Yes, I have a few items of value in my home – the odd heirloom that's come our way or a piece that has accumulated its worth quite by chance – but for the most part, what you see here are items I have collected over the years that have simply caught my eye and appealed to my evolving aesthetic: a pink flamingo that serves no purpose other than to make me smile when I see it each morning; a 1920s lamp Danny and I found in Clignancourt market on a romantic trip to Paris – which I then forced him carry back to London on the Eurostar because we realised we couldn't

LEFT Sometimes when I see something that really makes me smile, I simply just have to have it and that was the case with this pink flamingo I found on Golborne Road. It wasn't expensive, but I couldn't resist it and carried it home on the train, which was met with a few raised eyebrows from some of my fellow passengers – but it was worth it!

RIGHT I bought the bed for this spare room from a shop in Notting Hill over twenty years ago and then got a carpenter to make four-poster poles for it. I painted it white when we moved here, draping it with lace. The wallpaper is an exquisitely pretty print called Bradenham, from Nicholas Herbert. I wanted to give this room a feminine and romantic feel. Curtains by Hillarys, velvet chairs, fringed lamps and a chandelier bought from an antiques shop in Warminster help achieve that look.

afford the shipping cost (not so romantic!) – my assortment of mismatched china bought lucky-dip style from car boot sales, which, nevertheless, proudly adorns my table on the best of occasions; my animal-print cushions; my gypsy piano shawls; swathes of vintage lace.

These are all items and pieces that have no intrinsic value to anyone but myself, but when put together, against the backdrop of a house like this, they are for me what faded glamour is all about.

Rustic Faded Glamour

If there is one item Susie Forbes would save from the flames should her beautiful country house suddenly catch fire, then it would be the wonderfully quirky china dog lamp that takes pride of place in her living room. 'Well, I suppose at a push, I'd rescue the children first,' she laughs. 'But that lamp has a very special place in my heart. There was a moment last year when the Christmas tree inevitably came crashing down at a pivotal point in the proceedings, taking most of the room with it, needless to say, my first hysterical reaction was: "someone save the lamp!"'

Deliciously whimsical as the foot-high lamp is – a gift from her husband, the designer Bill Amberg – it isn't, perhaps, an object one would imagine being one of the Ambergs' prized possessions. For those not familiar with the couple, let me explain: Bill is one of the most respected names in British design, famous for his work in leather craft. Susie, in turn, is a highly successful magazine editor, having enjoyed tenures at *Elle*, *Vogue* and *Easy Living* before setting up the Condé Nast College of Fashion & Design. As such, you'd imagine them living the minimal, achingly cool urban dream – all white walls, clean lines and bespoke furniture. Which they do, when in London. But, when it comes to country living at the retreat they share with their three daughters, all that goes out of their beautiful stone mullioned windows. Think large groaning sofas, vintage wallpapers, flagstone floors and wood-burning stoves. Throw in a little Colefax and Fowler, china figurines and stuffed birds, and you're starting to get the picture. A bucolic dream far removed from their weekday existence in the busy metropolis.

The couple first chanced upon the house fifteen years ago and bought it in an attempt to prise their daughters away from the trudge of London weekends spent on play dates, playgrounds and screen time so they could

LEFT The Ambergs' much-loved porcelain dog lamp takes pride of place in the living room of the couple's thirteenth-century country retreat. It was an acquisition from the vintage emporium Les Couilles du Chien, on London's Golborne Road.

OVERLEAF Colour is added to the living room by the pink velvet chaise longue and a pair of blue-fringed chairs that the Ambergs bought for just £20 each on Portobello Road in London. The wood-burning stove was designed by Bill to replace an open fire grate which kept losing heat.

give them a taste of a country childhood. Built in 1260, with its mullioned windows, stone floors, timber beams and historic features, there was no denying its charm when they first got the property details from the estate agents. What they weren't told, however, was that there was a train line – quite literally – running down the end of their garden. But, by then it was too late, they had fallen in love with the property. 'I think trains are actually quite romantic, I like to think it's a bit *Railway Children*,' Susie explains, 'when guests first come here I'm sure they think the Polar Express is about to carve its way into the house – but we're all so used to it it's really not an issue.'

They made few structural changes to the house, other than to give the downstairs a more open-plan feel and to open up an attic space so the girls could have a vast den to hang out in. Windows have been left uncovered by either curtains or shutters to make the most of their aesthetic and the views of the surrounding countryside. To compensate for the loss of heat, Bill designed a vast wood-burning stove for the living room and also built an outdoor oven as the couple love to entertain. A talented chef, Bill thinks nothing of knocking up lunch for 30 or so people at the weekend and at New Year they seamlessly hosted a party for 100 guests. Bearing all this in mind, the kitchen is very much the hub of the house and to make it feel more welcoming they switched the original kitchen door for a stable door with a glass window. 'Not only did that create more light,' Susie explains, 'but I love the idea of people arriving for lunch or dinner and seeing where we all are. It's more inviting.'

When it came to decorating, they turned to their great friend Frances Penn. The daughter of the celebrated interiors guru David Mlinaric and a respected designer in her own right, Frances helped them choose fabrics and wallpapers that were traditional yet quirky. The upstairs spare bedroom has been papered in a vibrant green to create a dark Narnia-style forest haven. A family bathroom with a beautiful bevelled mirror is softened with a chintz from Colefax and Fowler to give it a traditional feel and a downstairs bathroom is livened up by a loud, floral American vintage wallpaper.

RIGHT Arranged on top of the 1930s glass table – with its metal and enamel flower stand – is a selection of vintage glasses the couple have owned for years, as well as a glass box that was a gift from their friend, the designer Solange Azagury-Partridge.

OVERLEAF A bright green wallpaper from Zoffany called Richmond Park lines the walls of the spare bedroom to create a Narnia-like feeling. It's set off by a striking headboard designed by Frances Penn with the upholsterers Hossack & Gray, covered in a red Kate Forman fabric called Pandora Red Floral. The velvet nursing chair is an heirloom from Bill's side. The floral picture on the stone mantelpiece is a gift from Christopher and Suzanne Sharp, founders of The Rug Company and close friends of the Ambergs.

They have furnished the house with finds from flea markets and junk shops, pieces that would never have fitted in their west London home – such as the 1930s glass flower table in their living room. They sourced the kitchen table from Suffolk. 'It's actually an old pub table because we needed something narrow for the space, and it's the perfect fit,' Susie says. Here they have also found a home for numerous family heirlooms – such as a velvet nursing chair that belonged to Bill's father and various knick-knacks that, again, wouldn't have worked in London. Bulging sofas have been covered in old flour sacks and dressed with cushions from The Rug Company. A kitchen dresser, which they inherited with the house and was once a dated brown colour, has been given a new lease on life with a simple lick of bright blue-green paint.

And then, of course, we have the china dog lamp. Bill bought it as a 'friend' for Susie's china cat lamp, which adorns another table in the living room. He said he simply couldn't resist it when he saw it sitting in the window of a decorative antiques emporium on Golborne Road in London. The name of the shop was Les Couilles du Chien – which, as far as Susie is concerned the lamp certainly is, and it would be the one item I'd also choose to rescue from the flames should their beautiful retreat ever have the misfortune of being set alight.

Colourful Faded Glamour

LEFT Solange Azagury-Partridge's use of bold colour, rich textiles and contrasting prints is on display at the far end of the living room where an antique Moroccan wall hanging is paired with a sofa covered in a traditional English floral chintz from Sanderson. Stone floors are covered with a patchwork of brightly-coloured rugs. The retro metal and enamel lamp at the side of the sofa was a find from London's Portobello Road.

OVERLEAF The living room – known as the 'Fire Room' because it boasts two fireplaces since Solange knocked two rooms into one – is a kaleidoscope of print. Gold silk adorns the wall on one side of the room, while the doorway has been lined with fabric from Manuel Canovas and is hung with an embroidered Indian curtain, which acts as a draught excluder. Artworks by Peter Blake and a contemporary print from an artist in Ibiza add further zest to the room.

If you are ever in need of an injection of colour on a cold, wet winter's night, then I suggest you inveigle an invitation to the three-bedroom country cottage where the designer Solange Azagury-Partridge sets up home on weekends, high days and holidays. Set in one of the most picturesque villages in the West Country, this is one of the most delightful cottages I have ever visited. Aside from the charm of the building itself with its tiny turret and beautiful walled garden, it's what lies inside that will make your spirits soar as she opens her baby pink front door and ushers you in from the cold.

Given that she is one of the most respected jewellery designers of her generation – some of her most exquisite pieces are on display at the Victoria and Albert Museum in London and the Musée des Arts Décoratifs in Paris, and she is also renowned for her interiors collections – you would expect Solange to know a thing or two about colour. But in this small space she takes her palette to another level, creating a home that is warm and inviting even on the most drab of days.

Solange and her husband Murray fell in love with the 100-year-old property more than a decade ago while visiting friends in Somerset. At the time, they wanted to create a nest that they and their children could seek refuge in, away from the big smoke of London. The brief was simple – she wanted it to feel like a home, rather than a weekend cottage, and it had to be comfortable, warm and welcoming.

By knocking down a couple of walls in the downstairs of the house and expanding the kitchen space into an outbuilding so they could comfortably seat ten people for gatherings, they have achieved this. At the core of the house is what Solange and her family call the Fire Room. 'It got that name because we have fireplaces at both ends of the room – which we gained by

LEFT A further living room – used as a snug when the family want to relax in front of the TV – is covered in a William Morris fabric and the star-print rug comes from Solange's own collection. The woodwork throughout the house is painted the prettiest of pinks and here the shutters keep out the cold at night. The leather sofa is from Lisson Grove in London and the bamboo desk is from OKA, which Solange customised by painting it black.

RIGHT An Eames-style chair and footstool have been updated with a botanical-print fabric from Sweden. 'I doubt very much it is real Eames because I picked up for £100,' laughs Solange.

OVERLEAF, LEFT AND RIGHT An umbrella stand has been covered in fabric from Biba. The hallway leads into the kitchen, which has been extended so that it can comfortably seat ten for dinner.

knocking a wall down and opening up the room,' she says. 'On a cold day, we light them both and hunker in here to read, talk and watch movies, and it's where we entertain when we aren't in the kitchen.' Key to her design plan was comfort, so everywhere you look are overstuffed sofas and day-beds waiting to be snuggled up on. 'When I'm here it's all about relaxing – I spend quite a lot of the time here horizontal, I'm not ashamed to say!' she laughs. These sofas and chairs are covered in a giddy array of colourful fabrics and throws that Solange has been collecting for years. 'I have piles and piles of fabric,' she says. 'I buy them on a whim – sometimes from abroad, often

LEFT The house is filled with sofas as Solange, by her own admission, likes to spend quite a lot of her time in the country 'lying horizontal'. Though reupholstered in the most divine chintz florals and bright ikats, she bought most of them from IKEA. 'They were very good value and I think they are exceptionally comfortable.'

RIGHT A pretty fuchsia toile de Jouy has been used in the hallways of the ground floor and also in the downstairs bathroom, where Solange has used the same print to create curtains to hide the utility cupboard and 'all the family junk'. The pink of the toile clashes beautifully with the golden silk used in the living room. 'I like it when colours and patterns meet and come together,' she says.

online, or I find them in markets. I never have a plan for their use, it will just come to me while I'm doing up a room and I'll seek one out that I think fits.'

Solange doesn't like to conform to the rules. In a corner of the living room, for example, a sofa covered in a flowery chintz from Sanderson sits happily at right angles to one dressed in an ikat print. Mismatched rugs from Morocco form a colourful patchwork across the central living spaces. A heavy, embroidered, mirrored curtain serves as a draft excluder over the front door; a wild, boldly coloured Swedish fabric has been used to cover an Eames-style chair and footstool in their snug. 'It was covered in black leather

LEFT Solange has created a real stairway to heaven with rainbow shades of carpet – not only has it created an incredible gem-like feature out of this delightful spiral, but it was a clever way of using off-cuts of carpet.

RIGHT The studded sofa in the hallway is part of a pair she bought from eBay and had recovered in vibrant yellow velvet. She built the cupboards in the hallway, again painted baby pink, to maximise storage. The rug, like many in the house, came from Morocco.

OVERLEAF Each of the three bedrooms in the property has a double and a single bed so the house can be filled to the brim over weekends and holidays. Contrasting fabrics line the walls: 'that's often because I simply don't have enough of one fabric to finish a room,' she explains, 'but I also like the contrast and it can make a room feel cosier.'

originally, which didn't work for me. Now it makes me smile and want to just sink into it in the evening.'

Suffice it to say, Solange loves her fabric – to such an extent that almost every single room is covered in it. 'I love using fabric on walls, because it feels not only quite luxurious, but it's warm and also creates a depth of sound in a room – a soft echo that you wouldn't get from papers or paint.' And what I love here is that she hasn't been afraid to mix these fabrics up – so they are often not only contrasting with each other, but going head to head in a riot of colour and pattern. 'That's actually for practical and

LEFT Colourful textiles – including a Suzani embroidered fabric on the wall – contrast beautifully with old-fashioned chintz cushions in this bedroom.

RIGHT The family bathroom – one of the few rooms in the house not to have been lined with fabric – is papered in a palm-print Martinique design that Solange saw and fell in love with at the Beverly Hills Hotel. The rolltop bath came with the house. 'That was lucky, because I have no idea how we would have got a bath up the spiral staircase!'

economic reasons,' she admits. 'As I often don't have enough of one fabric so have to use another, but I like the effect in a house like this.'

All the woodwork in the house has been painted the most enchanting shade of baby pink. And on the spiral turret staircase leading up to the first floor, she has been even braver with her use of colour by covering each step in a different shade of carpet, creating a magical rainbow to take you up to bed – a real stairway to heaven.

A yellow velvet studded sofa that she bought as a pair from eBay for £100 (she loves a bargain, as do I, which is why she is woman after my own heart)

LEFT AND RIGHT The
master bedroom – including
the sloping ceiling, far wall
and bedlinen – is covered in
a wonderfully old-fashioned
antique oak print, which is
contrasted with panels of
the Manuel Canovas fabric
Solange used downstairs in
the Fire Room.

clashes against the shocking pink toile de Jouy she has lined the hallway
and downstairs bathroom with. Fabrics from William Morris and Liberty have
been used to create warmth and cosiness in rooms where all anyone wants
to do is kick their shoes off and relax.

   This is certainly a house that I would like to spend some serious horizontal
time in, as Solange's bold use of colour is full of wit and wonder and brings a
smile to your face. 'But that's the thing about colour – we all need a bit of it in
our lives,' she says. 'And for me, quite frankly, I can never have enough of it.'

Chic Faded Glamour

Romantic, dreamy, luxurious, ornate and above all, quintessentially British – these are just some of the adjectives that spring to mind when thinking about the creations of the fashion designer Alice Temperley, but they could just as easily be applied in turn to Cricket Court, the eight-bedroom Regency mansion in the heart of Somerset where she resides when not running her eponymous and much-coveted label from London.

Built in the early nineteenth century, Cricket Court – set in five acres of land – is the most extraordinary house. When Alice was once asked to describe it, she joked that it reminded her of 'an M.C. Escher wedding cake', as a result of its position on top of a hill, the long French windows that wrap around the ground floor, its grand pillared portico and prism-shaped roof. Deliciously whimsical to look at it may be, but it is also a house steeped in history. It stands on land that William the Conqueror gave to his brother and it was here that the Canadian newspaper magnate Lord Beaverbrook resided during the Second World War, where he is said to have entertained Churchill in the house's domed library with its crowning oculus. There is also an original Tudor bear pit within the grounds, which now – fitted with a makeshift dancefloor – has a new, more entertaining and less grisly lease on life, serving as Cricket Court's very own nightclub.

Those familiar with Alice Temperley's designs will recognise her deep fascination with heritage. Modern and edgy as her creations are – adored by some of the most stylish women in the world, from the Duchess of Cambridge to Beyoncé – they defy trends by being classically timeless at the same time, and this sense of style is reflected in her country house, where she playfully mixes the old with the new. Giant disco balls hang from original plaster roses on the ceiling and black-and-white photographs and

LEFT An aubergine velvet curtain, finished with a silk print from the Temperley archive and designed and made by Alice herself, frames one of the many French windows of this Regency property. On the chair is her son Fox's guitar, a find from London's Golborne Road.

OVERLEAF The living room – one of the property's three reception rooms – is also painted aubergine, a colour she loves because of its earthiness. The designer collects screens, often mounting them on the wall, and this one was bought in Hong Kong when she was living there. The model ship on the mantelpiece was a gift from Alice to her son, because as she says: 'all little boys like pirates at some point!'

LEFT Alice is a collector of textiles and vintage clothes, which you will find artfully draped across the house. This antique bolero – an original Spanish bullfighting jacket – was bought from a dealer on Portobello Road in London.

RIGHT A hand-cut crystal glass and antique decanter rest on one of the many design books from which Alice derives inspiration for her collections.

OVERLEAF When she isn't entertaining family and friends, the dining room, which features a mural by the artist Frederick Wimsett – seen here reflected in the vintage mirror – doubles as a studio when she needs to spread out. The pendant light was bought years ago on a trip to Paris.

contemporary art line the walls of wood-panelled reception rooms. In the dining room she has commissioned the artist Frederick Wimsett – with whom she has since collaborated in the decoration of her London flagship store – to paint a beautiful Chinoiserie-style peacock mural, which, in turn, sets off the room's original Regency coffered ceiling.

Alice is a great standard-bearer for all things British, which is fitting when you consider that she was awarded an MBE for her services to the fashion industry in 2011, when she was only in her thirties. Images of the Union Jack are a recurring theme throughout the house – even her freestanding rolltop

LEFT Built in the 1800s on the foundations of a castle, the house has many architectural features. The arches, pillars, alcoves and flagstone floor, seen here in the hallway, all contribute to the sense of grandeur. 'Its beautiful lines defy logic,' Alice explains, 'it's a bit like an Italian court – in Somerset!'

RIGHT Jars of jewel-like beads, brightly-coloured buttons and sparkly sequins line the surfaces of Alice's home.

bath – embellished by her own fair hand with a mosaic of disco mirrors – stands on a plinth decorated with the flag.

Alice isn't afraid of colour, either – rooms are painted in rich hues: dark aubergine, robin's egg blue and dusky pink, and are made even warmer with vibrant rugs and textiles. Against this backdrop, she has adorned the house with eclectic finds from the local flea markets: twinkling candelabras, vintage glassware, bespoke china and stacks of rare books are some of the treasures that Alice's eye is drawn to when she's trawling markets and shops, either at home or on her travels.

LEFT The stuffed rabbit, mounted on the wall and decorated with necklaces, simply amuses Alice – she also has a stuffed fox and a moose, which she has adorned with a tiara.

RIGHT The art deco glass table in this hallway came from Les Couilles du Chien on Golborne Road in London.

OVERLEAF Alice's sumptuously curved bedroom, with its domed ceiling, has been painted a heritage dusky pink, mixed by a friend in the local village who specialises in historic paint colours. The ER royal cypher above her bed is festooned with Union Jack flags – a nod to her sense of patriotism. 'I love the flag,' she explains, 'and I love the Queen!'

What I love about this house is, that despite the grandeur of the building itself – which in other hands could look austere and formal – Alice has, with her inherent romantic aesthetic, created a whimsical, enchanted world here. (I doubt very much that it had such a feeling when Lord Beaverbrook was in residence). Yes, it's palatial, but at the same time it's very much a home. It's the kind of house where you'd feel equally as comfortable arriving for lunch in your Wellington boots after a long dog walk, as wafting into the dining room on a warm summer's evening in a sequined dress, with a glass of something cold and sparkling in hand.

LEFT An antique crystal beaded sconce has been livened up by a jauntily-placed vintage appliquéd shade.

RIGHT The gilt-edged striped chair was found, along with the cushions, on Alice's travels.

OVERLEAF Alice's own bathroom – with disco balls and a mirrored rolltop bath set upon a Union Jack plinth – is wonderfully quirky, but this downstairs bathroom has a more traditional feel. It's been painted the same dusky pink as her bedroom. The door in the curved wall leads into a walk-in wardrobe.

And that's exactly the feeling Alice wanted to create when she bought the property in 2010. Raised on her parents' cider farm along with her three siblings, despite her achingly cool credentials in the fashion world she is very much a Somerset girl at heart, and she wanted a country retreat where she could recreate her idyllic rural childhood for her son, Fox. And while this isn't her primary residence, it's a house that is very much about family and friends, where children are encouraged to run wild. Saturday nights are heavenly affairs filled with people and music, which she is passionate about – so much so the house even boasts its own piano room.

LEFT AND RIGHT A light and airy guest bedroom is given a burst of colour with red velvet curtains and an emerald green bedspread. The bed, a French reproduction, was bought online. All the mirrors came from Paris and the antique lacquered bedside table was another acquisition from Hong Kong, when Alice lived there.

On Sundays, there are long lunches where family and local friends are encouraged to bring a dish, washed down with cider from the Temperleys' farm. Don't be surprised if a four-legged guest is present, either – Alice is the proud owner of two alpacas and her neighbour's miniature donkeys can often be found wandering into the drawing room. Her annual summer fête has become legendary, it's where artists, musicians and other creatives gather in the lantern-festooned garden before hitting the bear pit for dancing at sunset.

But just as this house is very much about people – and parties – it's also Alice's sanctuary, a place where she seeks refuge from the day-to-day

LEFT Old meets new in the domed library, where a picture of the model Sophie Dahl standing in front of the Union Jack takes pride of place on the panelled wall. The artwork, which is embroidered over, was made by Alice for The Circle, a charity for women's equality founded by Annie Lennox. 'I love doing projects like that,' Temperley says.

RIGHT The exquisite blue Venetian glass chandelier in the hallway was bought in a souk in Morocco ten years ago. Alice fell in love with it and had it shipped back to London.

demands of running her hugely successful brand. A spacious, airy workroom is filled with swatches of cloth and jars of sequins and beads, tables stacked high with piles of her sketchbooks and the fashion and photography tomes she uses for reference. Dressmakers' mannequins are dotted around the house, testament to the fact that it's here, at Cricket Court, that she derives much of her inspiration and puts pen to paper in the first stages of her delectable designs.

This house, to me, is the epitome of chic, faded glamour. It's a house of stories – old and new – and is very much Alice Temperley's own Wonderland.

Urban Faded Glamour

When Danny and I first decided to uproot our family from London to the countryside all those years ago, it's fair to say that most of our friends thought we'd never go the distance.

But fifteen years on, here we are and despite a couple of wobbles along the way, I can honestly say that not a day goes by when we don't wake up and thank the gods that we made the great escape. Yes, there are moments when I look back fondly on our times in Camden in our beautiful white stucco house. Days when I'm secretly pleased that I have to come to town for work and can sneak off to my favourite Japanese restaurant for lunch, or to meet an old friend for tea at a gallery. But, there is nothing I like more than coming home. It's taken me a while, but I've realised that I'm a country girl at heart.

Suffice it to say, if you wanted me to up and move from the sticks back to London, you'd have to take me kicking and screaming, unless you gave me the keys to the London home of Marianne Cotterill. Then I would go silently, happily and freely, without the slightest of protests, because that's how much I adore this extraordinary property in the middle of the big smoke.

Let me explain why: Marianne Cotterill, with her keen eye, her exquisite taste and her innate sense of style, has created a home that most of us would give our eye teeth to live in. A leading interiors stylist and designer, she effortlessly creates beautiful spaces that are used as backdrops for magazine editorials and advertising campaigns. Her client list, from private to commercial projects, is broad and throughout her career she has worked alongside some of the biggest names and brands in interiors, fashion and design: Farrow & Ball, *Vogue* and Bottega Veneta, to name just a few.

Marianne doesn't just decorate rooms – it's far more than that. What she does is create storyboards within spaces, whether that's for private or

LEFT The beautiful hand-painted wall in Marianne Cotterill's reception room – which she created on a whim and in just a day – that turns this corner into her very own rose garden. The heart-shaped chair was a find from a flea market in Paris and was later reupholstered in yellow silk. The 1970s table and lamp are from Belgium and she found the ornamental horse in a market in California.

LEFT It's a property full of beautiful and interesting objects, and many have been customised by Marianne herself, such as the candle sconce above the radiator. It was in desperate need of attention, but rather than buy new shades for it, she simply painted them with a vibrant green emulsion.

RIGHT The house retains many of its original features – from parquet flooring, to ceiling plasterwork, cornices, picture and dado rails, to this quite stunning hand-painted stained-glass double portico, with a tiled floor.

OVERLEAF Pictures of no particular value, chosen simply because Marianne likes them, are given ornate, vintage frames to help them stand out. They are often hung way above eye level, because she likes to view them from different angles – when she is lying on a sofa or they are reflected in a mirror.

commercial purposes, or simply for her own delight and amusement in her London home.

And her house, a vast Victorian mansion in northwest London – thanks to her ingenuity – runs as a very successful go-to location for fashion shoots, advertising campaigns and film and television productions. Walking through the stained-glass double portico which takes you into the main hallway of the property, you can fully understand why it is such a sought-after location. This is a house of grand proportions on the Victorian scale. Three large receptions, which lead into one another, are light-filled and airy thanks

LEFT Marianne uses the house as a location for shoots, so most of the reception rooms have to be painted shades of white to act as a backdrop. But in the hallways, she has been able to express her love of colour. She has used a bold green-blue on the main landing and hallway. Above the radiator is a framed panel of wallpaper by the designer Florence Broadhurst.

RIGHT There are three reception rooms on the ground floor, which flow into one another – this one is divided by elegant French doors which allow the light to shine through from the front to the back of the house.

to high ceilings and long sash windows. Landings in the house are in some cases are so spacious that they act as small rooms or can carry a large, inviting sofa. 'I do love a sofa on a landing!' Marianne laughs. 'I spend so much of my working day on my feet, so I quite like the idea of having a sneaky little sit-down when I'm between floors.' A charming conservatory at the back of the house leads you into an oasis of a garden, generous by London standards.

Such is the stature of the property, it's easy to see why photographers and art editors alike flock to use this house as a prime location, but it's what

LEFT AND RIGHT With high ceilings, the house lends itself to overhead lighting and Marianne has used chandeliers to set the mood. 'There was another reason behind that,' she confesses, 'I ordered a job lot of chandeliers – boxes full of them, which I bought for nothing. Some were great, others not, but they found a home here.' In the foreground is a Murano glass ceiling lamp she found in a junk shop in Belgium.

Marianne has created within its walls that really takes your breath away. Thanks to her style and pure genius, there isn't a nook or cranny in this house that doesn't catch your eye. Even the way she has hung her pictures is interesting. Debunking the common decorative myth that pictures should always be hung at eye level, here you'll spot a portrait hanging high above a door, way beyond a picture rail, or far below a chair rail. 'I like doing that,' she says, 'because often when – let's say – you are lying on a sofa, it will catch your eye and you can have a really good look at it, or it might be reflected back to you in a mirror, talking to you when you least expect it.'

LEFT A view from the other side of the hand-painted wall in the reception room. The pink day-bed from B&B Italia – surrounded by a pair of 1970s lamps and tables – is adorned with silk cushions. Hanging above the daybed is an artwork by her friend, Iain R Webb.

RIGHT Marianne has a fascination with portraits, and this one caught her eye because it reminded her of her daughter.

She enjoys turning things on their heads, but not in a contrived way, simply because after a lot of consideration, she'll decide it simply looks better. She mixes styles with ease. Mingles her more 'trashy' finds (her words, not mine) with her more high-end collectibles. And she finds joy in the simplest of objects: she'll take a freestanding radiator, for example, and just as the rest of us would start to think about distressing it so it can blend into our homes and look more vintage, she'll make it a feature, painting it a bright Lego green, as she has done in her dining area. It's a house full of stories – tales of the unexpected.

LEFT AND RIGHT The conservatory, which leads on to Marianne's beautiful garden, is one of my favourite spaces in the house. The beams have been painted a mottled green so it serves as a seamless extension between house and garden. The beautiful tiles she sourced from Belgium are delightful and the vast orange-fringed lamp by Honoré Déco simply makes this room.

When Marianne and her husband Terry first bought the house, it wasn't with the intention of turning it into a business. They gravitated towards it because with five children and their dogs they needed the space. While size mattered in this respect, Marianne did wonder, even with her prowess as a stylist, how she was ever going to fill it. 'We came from quite a small house before and it was slightly overwhelming when I thought about how we were going to make it work, but things just gradually began to evolve over the years,' she says.

Built in 1882, the house was in good condition when they moved in. The only structural work they did was to knock through a downstairs wall so that

a small kitchenette could blossom into a vast living and dining space. But the house retained most of its period features – parquet floors, fireplaces, sash windows and the stained-glass porch. 'To be honest, I wasn't so sure about that, and I'm still not,' Marianne admits, 'but friends always comment on it and as it's made from hand-painted stained glass I think it would be sacrilege to take a sledgehammer to it. I'm all for change and not living with things that you don't like, but I think that would be a step too far!'

What has made this house become so magical is really down to Marianne's own instinctive creativity. While some of us – who like to think

ABOVE What I love in this kitchen is the way Marianne has injected a burst of colour into the room by painting the panel above the dining-room cabinet and the radiator the same emerald green. The long 1970s cabinet came from a contact in Belgium.

LEFT What could have been a dull hallway at the back of the house has been given a life of its own with this shimmering wallpaper from Florence Broadhurst. The fabulous 1960s lamp gives the space an even more glamorous feel and the portrait on the wall – which Marianne later had framed – was bought for the staggering sum of just £3.

RIGHT An upstairs landing which is currently serving as a storage space for Marianne's many finds. The portrait of the waving bride is a 1960s artwork for an advertising campaign for the now-defunct BOAC airlines.

we appreciate the finer things in life – might be tempted to throw money at something beautiful, what she does is invest both her time and talent to achieve that look.

Take the first reception room, which has been painted by her own fair hand on a whim. Enchanted by a detail of a watercolour of a rose that she found, she photocopied it, cut it out, transferred it to the wall, painting over and washing it. It was an experiment and she meant to stop there, but didn't – and by the end of the day the whole room had been transformed into her very own rose garden, an effect that would have cost the rest of us a vast amount of money to achieve. In the hallway is a small brass sconce she thought looked a little tired as a result of its stained shades, but rather than trawl the antiques shops or even the internet to source new ones, she simply broke open a pot of green emulsion paint and took her brush to them. 'It took all of twenty minutes,' she says breezily. And when it comes to art, she has the same approach. Though there are some wonderful pieces in her house, she'll admit that quite a lot of the works you see are just images that she has been drawn to, bought for a song, but cleverly framed. 'I'm quite drawn to portraits of people I don't know. I just find them fascinating, wondering who they were and how they lived,' she says.

Of course, not all of us are as blessed with Marianne's creative skills – she did, after all, train at Chelsea College of Art – but we can learn a lot from her in terms of buying and sourcing objects. Because of the nature of her job she is constantly at flea markets and sales looking for finds for her clients. Often she'll buy something not really knowing what to do with it, but she'll save it for another day, another set or room. 'I don't get worried about that because I know I'll always find a place for it, and I don't think we should get too attached to things. I think we should be free to change rooms and looks when we can to suit our lives and how we live,' she explains. 'The one tip I would give to anyone who is scouting the markets is not to buy something just for the sake of it. You need to think about how you're going to live with that piece down the line, even if you don't use it immediately. My rule when I'm out and about is to find things that really make me smile.'

RIGHT A generously-proportioned landing between the ground and first floors – with original stained-glass windows – is majestic in its grandeur and is large enough to fit a Chesterfield sofa, perfect for Marianne, who jokes that when she's been on her feet all day she quite likes the idea of a sit-down between floors.

LEFT A sense of pure theater has been created in Marianne's bedroom with sumptuous deep pink curtains, trimmed with pompoms. 'When it's sunny and the light shines through them, it's as if the room's on fire,' she says.

RIGHT The charming sofa is one of my favourite pieces in the house and one I keep begging Marianne to give me. The top of the sofa had to be completely reupholstered, but rather than cover the whole sofa, Marianne has kept its original Victorian fabric on the base.

OVERLEAF The bed is French and has been upholstered in a Chinoiserie fabric, and her bedside lamps are from Honoré Déco. The marble sink in the bedroom is original to the house.

Some of her greatest finds have come from the flea markets of Belgium, which she adores. When she was redecorating her kitchen, she had originally planned to use polished concrete for the floor, until a friend living in Belgium tipped her off that one of her favourite cafés was about to close and the building was to be gutted. Remembering its pretty tiled floors, without a moment of hesitation, she made a call and within a matter of weeks they arrived at her front door. She set about positioning them tile-by-tile across the floor like a jigsaw. She wasn't entirely sure if she would have enough, but she got there in the end. 'I was in a bit of a panic thinking I didn't have

LEFT Marianne's bedroom is part of a set of rooms that leads into a bathroom, then into a further master bedroom, also complete with its original sink – which once probably served as a 'his and hers' suite.

RIGHT The floral bedlinen comes from the fashion and design house, Preen.

enough of the right colour – so what I did was divide them up and create a border, a bit like a giant tiled rug.'

The only drawback of letting the house out for shoots, Marianne says, is that she has to be somewhat restrained with her use of colour on the walls, especially in the main living spaces, as clients tend to prefer them blank. To get round this conundrum, she has been bold in the areas where they don't shoot, using dark blue-greys in the hallways and the landings, for example. She also argues that these colours look better in areas which are naturally deprived of light. 'Paint it white and I promise you it will just look gloomier

LEFT Towards the top of the house is Marianne's son's bedroom and it's still very much 'work in progress', as she adapts the house now her children are grown-up. 'The headboard certainly needs to be covered,' she says, 'but I love making changes to rooms since that's part of my job, I'm very open like that.'

RIGHT The chandelier reflected in the mirror was made for Marianne by a sculptor in Brittany and the antique mirror itself is French.

rather than lighter.' In other areas of the house she has turned to wallpaper to insert a little drama into her home, such as the metallic patterned wallpaper by the late Australian designer Florence Broadhurst, which she has used in a hallway at the back of the house.

'The one good thing I'd say about renting your house out for shoots is that you can be a little freer when it comes to decoration,' Marianne says. 'Because I'm constantly having to move things around, remove pictures from the walls – even repaint them – or deal with the odd breakage, it keeps me on my toes and makes me see the house in a whole new light each time.'

Sophisticated Faded Glamour

When I asked Helen Kenny to describe the style of her country house she summed it up perfectly: 'It's a bit of a mix – think 1770s smooching with some 1970s French chic thrown in.' Walking through the rooms of this traditional Grade II listed old rectory – a six-bedroom long house, very much in the West Country tradition – not only is this description amusing, but it's also spot-on. It's traditional, yes, as she and her husband Jamie have spent years lovingly restoring the original features of the house that previous owners had either neglected or rather sacrilegiously torn out. But the process of their renovation and the pieces they have furnished it with make it ooze with style. This is a house where I would want to while away my time in Helen's dressing room, having had a long soak in her boudoir-like bathroom, before heading downstairs into their impossibly chic (for the country) drawing room to put on a little light mood music – possibly something by Charles Trenet – as I contemplate what to cook for supper in their kitchen, which, with its stone floor, pale-blue Aga and large welcoming table is just the way I would want to an end a day, over a steaming hot bowl of food.

Now, before I carry on extolling the virtues of this house, I have to make a confession: the reason why this house could be a home-from-home for me is that it actually was once my home. Danny and I lived here for a year, having stumbled on the property and fallen in love with it and its magnificent gardens. We spent many happy times here and had big plans for it, but unfortunately, due to geography alone (my carbon footprint for the school run was sinful), we reluctantly left a house we loved. But any remorse we felt as we packed our possessions into yet another removal van was eased by the fact that Helen, a producer, and Jamie, who is the co-founder of a digital marketing agency, had been thrown the keys. They wanted to

LEFT A dusky red chaise longue, found in an antiques shop in Brighton, brings a touch of theatre to Helen Kenny's dressing room, which leads directly off the master bedroom. Floor-to-ceiling armoires line the room, the doors fitted with glass windows. A pink glass chandelier hanging overhead gives the room a feminine look.

OVERLEAF A bold curved 1970s sofa from Geoffrey Harcourt – which has been brought back to life by Karen Naismith Robertson in Frome, Somerset – takes centre stage in the Kennys' drawing room. The soft palette, from the panelled walls to the painted floor, creates a room that is elegant and serene, while the glass tables and Anglepoise lamps lend a contemporary edge.

LEFT Used throughout the house, luxurious velvets add flashes of colour against the pale backdrop of the walls.

RIGHT In the Kennys' en-suite bathroom, walls have been lined with panels of exquisite lace from the renowned weavers Morton, Young and Borland of Scotland in collaboration with Timorous Beasties. With an antique gilt mirror hanging over the darkly painted rolltop bath, this room is boudoir chic at its best.

OVERLEAF Wanting to make the most of the original features of the kitchen – the stone floor, the charming window seat – the Kennys have filled it with a wonderful mix of old tables, cupboards and chairs, sourced locally and in France, giving it a shabby chic feeling that makes it incredibly homely. On the wooden bench sits Ardghal, the family's Irish Terrier.

create a family home outside of London for their two teenage children and, to quote them, their 'completely untrainable' Irish Terrier.

Though the house was far from being a wreck when they walked through the door in 2015, it did need some serious work and that's what they have done. They removed the rendering on the outside of the building, which had been painted white, to reveal the original stonework. The sprawling gardens, which had been vague areas of lawn, are now landscaped to create areas where you can appreciate different aspects of the countryside at varying times of day and they have created a stunning walled garden. An outbuilding

LEFT, RIGHT AND
OVERLEAF, LEFT A pair of
antique buttoned chairs covered
in powder blue velvet bring
a jolt of colour to the grand
hallway of the Georgian
property. To accentuate the
classic features, such as the
original panelling on the walls,
and to make the most of the
light which floods in from the
arched window on the first floor
landing, the couple have
painted the area an antique
white. A Roger Oates bordered
runner takes you up the stairs
to the first floor bedrooms.

that we had earmarked as a potential bedroom for my daughter Daisy –
which had only got as far as looking like a glorified shed-with-a-bed – has
been transformed into a suite of rooms that you'd be happy to pay hotel
prices for.

The drawing room – with its white walls, pale painted floorboards and retro
furniture – has a slightly decadent feel. But, at the heart of the house the
kitchen, which Helen describes as 'robust', is enough for all their needs.
The cushioned window seat under a mullioned window, bathed in sunlight
in the morning, is the perfect place for that first fix of daily caffeine.

RIGHT At the end of the hallway on the first floor is a spare bathroom, which has a distinctly Moroccan feeling to it. Ivory mosaic tiles cover the back wall, the sunken window has been dressed with vintage china, the surround of the bath painted a blue-green and covered in a mosaic-style paper by Louise Body, called Patchwork Jade. Antique crystal candle sconces line the walls, as well as the adjoining hallway.

OVERLEAF An old dressing screen – found in a brocante when the couple were holidaying in Northern France – has been cleverly used as an elegant headboard for the double bed in the panelled spare room. A hand-painted detail can be seen on the right.

This is a house of two halves – quite literally. The oldest part of the rectory dates back to 1620, so characteristic of that period, it has low ceilings and is quite dark, but the Kennys have enjoyed making that a feature, creating warm, cosy areas, perfect for a cold winter's night. On the south side of the property – which is Georgian – ceilings are high and it benefits from long sash windows. They have cleverly played with that by using a subtle palette of neutrals and pastels, pale textiles, clean lines and well-chosen furniture, and have created a completely different mood – calm, serene and elegant.

LEFT The lace curtain hanging over the pink rolltop bath comes from my own lace collection.

RIGHT What was once just an outbuilding has been transformed into a charming spare room. The cladding in the bedroom and adjacent bathroom is painted boards reclaimed from Old Albion in Bridport, Dorset.

It can be strange walking into a house where you once lived and seeing what others have done to it: how they've made their mark. While Helen and I have a similar aesthetic, what the couple have done here makes me stop in my tracks and wonder 'why didn't I think of that?' A niggling question in the back of my mind, vocalised loudly and rather unhelpfully by my children, who, when invited over to the Kennys for the first time, said, as Helen gave them the tour: 'Why didn't the house look like this when we lived here, Mum? It's so much nicer now!'

Vintage Faded Glamour

When the founders of Hauser & Wirth announced that they were planning to open a new gallery space in Somerset, eyebrows were raised. Could it really be that this cutting-edge contemporary art gallery – with a star roster of some of the greatest artists of our time such as Louise Bourgeois, Martin Creed, and Paul McCarthy – was about to set up shop in Somerset? With galleries in all the major art hubs around the world – London, Zürich and New York – they couldn't seriously be considering a major expansion near the market town of Bruton, in a derelict farm, down what was once just a very muddy lane, surely not.

Don't get me wrong, with its collection of independently run cafés, restaurants, and shops, Bruton is one of my favourite towns in the country and a lovely place to wile away your day. You come here to buy your bread from the bakery at The Chapel, visit the butcher, browse the bookshop and antiques shops – but would you come here to look at contemporary art?

Well, apparently that's exactly what you do, because since it first opened its doors to the public in 2014, Hauser & Wirth Somerset, with its gallery spaces, educational centre, stunning landscaped grounds designed by the Dutch master of garden design Piet Oudolf and its Roth Bar & Grill, has become a destination not just for the local community, but for visitors from all over the world.

But what draws me to the Somerset branch of Hauser & Wirth isn't its schedule of headline exhibitions, the restaurant or even the gardens – fabulous as they are – it's the six-bedroom farmhouse Durslade, which lies at the heart of this ambitious project.

Built in 1768, left untouched for over half a century, abandoned for ten years, and in a state of chronic disrepair, this little house was in serious need

LEFT The directors of Hauser & Wirth and architect and designer Luis Laplace have managed to celebrate the history of an old building while providing a background for the gallery's art collection. In the doorway from this bedroom, vintage floral wallpaper is combined with pale paint hues to create a tranquil feeling.

of some love and attention. Manuela and Iwan Wirth, founders of the gallery, were keen to inject a little love and cash into the property and bring it back to its former glory – with a contemporary twist – creating a house where artists in residence, critics, family and friends, as well as paying guests could stay when visiting the gallery. For the Wirths, this was almost a personal project, because having fallen in love with and moved to this part of the country over a decade ago, they wanted to give something back to the community.

Needing an architect with a sensitive eye to oversee the renovation, they turned to the acclaimed Paris-based Luis Laplace and persuaded him to come to England and wave his magic wand over this property. When he first visited the farmhouse, he came with a head full of ideas to restore, renovate and rejuvenate the house, creating a liveable space where contemporary art and tradition would be happy housemates. His initial plan was to paint the house in traditional heritage colours and lime washes in keeping with the history of the property, modernise the kitchen and put in a series of uniform, contemporary bathrooms to keep us demanding, modern paying guests happy. But, as soon as the builders started work that plan went straight up one of the many stone chimneypieces.

'As we stripped it back, the house gave us more and more information about its past,' he explains. 'And I was determined not to lose any of that – far from it – I wanted to play with that sense of heritage and expose the history of the house, while bringing it up to date.'

Peeling back the layers of wallpaper, paint and plaster, Laplace's heart began to sing, for as the builders worked through the house, these rooms – once dusty and blandly decorated – began to reveal a predominant colour in each – ochre, red, pale pink, sea green and dusky blue – and this was the palette he would then work from. He would use these colours throughout the house, whether painting a door or the hallway, or selecting the hand-dyed heavy linens used for the curtains and the soft furnishings. In some rooms, he decided to keep the original plasterwork exposed, believing that it told the story of the house. In others, walls are lined with pretty, mismatched vintage floral wallpapers. Such was his commitment to telling the story of the house and its past inhabitants, he even insisted the stickers on the walls, which must have been put up by the children who once lived here, were left

LEFT Throughout the house, furniture has been upholstered in heavy linens which have been hand-dyed to complement the colourways of each room – like this turquoise armchair. Curios such as this life-sized dog give the house a sense of quirkiness.

RIGHT The walls of the flagstoned hallway of the house have been stripped back to their former glory, while the row of Wellington boots available for guest use gives the house a homey feel when you enter the building.

intact in the living room and the attic bedroom. In the large spacious kitchen, a fake wall that probably dated back to renovations done in the sixties and had an unsightly electric bar heater hanging from it, was ripped down to reveal a huge stone hearth. Likewise, when they pulled up the faded, sticky linoleum flooring that covered the room, a beautiful and intact flagstone floor was discovered. This house, as far as Laplace was concerned, was a gift that just kept giving… and giving.

With so much character emerging from the house as the renovation progressed, Laplace abandoned all plans to give every room its hotel-suite-

LEFT At the heart of the house is the warm, spacious kitchen which has been refitted with cupboards from a local vintage boutique. During renovations, an enormous hearth fireplace and a beautifully preserved stone tile floor were revealed.

RIGHT An assortment of china plates sourced from local junk shops have been used to decorate the walls.

OVERLEAF A mix of pretty vintage wallpapers has been used to decorate this upstairs bedroom, its painted pink ceiling giving the room a cosy feeling. The framed acrylic painting on the far wall is by Phyllida Barlow and somehow, this work of contemporary art doesn't look at all out of place in what is essentially quite an old-fashioned room.

style bathrooms, as he knew that wouldn't work. Now, I can be a little quirky at times and don't think there should be dictates on taste, but when it comes to bathrooms I'm quite a traditionalist. Aside from my own copper bath, when it comes to my porcelain I'm a Burlington White girl through and through, or so I thought… for who knew I'd suddenly have a 'thing' for a coloured bathroom set! But here it is at Durslade in its full glory, for Laplace has taken those sherbet fittings and made them cool again. Pale blues, salmon pinks, yellows, avocado greens – all chosen to complement the decorating theme of each room. It's not just retro or kitsch, for by simply

LEFT Woodwork throughout the house has either been distressed, as here, or it has been painted in glossy sherbet shades or primary colours.

RIGHT A vintage pendant lamp and 1950s-style mirror give this bedroom the feeling of a bygone era, while a button chair upholstered in coral linen complements the pinks of the painted walls and the piece of art by Phyllida Barlow. Throughout the house, copper pipes have been left exposed.

replacing taps and swapping plastic toilet seats for black wooden ones, he's made these bathrooms joyously pretty and also saved huge amounts of money down the line, for such is our innate and snobbish distaste for coloured bathroom fittings that salvage yards are full of them and they can be purchased for next to nothing.

Once the backdrop of the house was completed, it was time to kit the house out. Art, needless to say, was to come from Hauser & Wirth's star artists. Some of the pieces in the house are provided on loan and displayed on rotation – photographs by Roni Horn, works by Phyllida Barlow, for

LEFT As Laplace stripped the walls back during the renovation, to his delight, he found a predominant colour in every room. In this bathroom, hues of blue were unveiled, which is why he chose the blue porcelain bathroom set and hung a framed butterfly collection, reflected here in the mirror.

RIGHT In the bedroom, a pretty, intricate floral wallpaper lines the walls.

OVERLEAF In another bedroom, the wallpaper is busier and its green and purple colours have been picked out for the curtains and used to reupholster the headboard of the brass bed.

example – the idea being that as much as this is a comfortable and stylish farmhouse, it is still very much an extension of the gallery. Other pieces are permanent and in some areas have been commissioned especially for Durslade. In the dining room, a striking geometric mural by the artist Guillermo Kuitca wraps around the walls. In one of the main double bedrooms a strip of vibrant blue, cheeky wallpaper designed by Paul McCarthy has been used. In the living room an installation by the artist Pipilotti Rist hangs from the ceiling: a chandelier made from glass, antique bottles and ornaments that lights up the room.

LEFT AND RIGHT One of the largest bedrooms in the house has been papered down one side with a rather cheeky wallpaper by the artist Paul McCarthy. The blue in the background of the paper is followed through in the rug and also the ceiling. The purple upholstered chairs are from Du Long et Du Lé in Belgium. The artwork on the wall is by Phyllida Barlow.

The art might have an international flavour, but when it comes to the rest of the house much of what you see here has been locally sourced. That wasn't only because the Wirths wanted to give back to the community and the surrounding counties, but because it was agreed by all involved that despite all its contemporary nods, Durslade should stay true to its roots and celebrate its life as a former working West Country farmhouse.

The charming collection of china that adorns the kitchen walls and its dresser came from flea markets and car boot sales in the area; lamps and curios from the shops of Frome; beds, mirrors, tables and chairs from local

LEFT An artwork by Rita
Ackermann entitled 'Fire
by Days' hangs in the red
hallway at Durslade, and
can be seen here from an
upstairs bathroom.

RIGHT In this suite of rooms,
pale green has been chosen
for the decorative palette.
The sink in the bathroom, the
painted ceiling – even
the bedside lamp – are all
in shades of this colour.

antiques sales; materials and wood from nearby reclamation yards; and they
also relied on the services of Phillips & Skinner, a treasure trove of vintage
furniture and finds, situated at the time, handily, just up the road on Bruton's
main street.

Durslade Farmhouse to me is a perfect example of vintage faded glamour
in so many respects. This is a renovation project that has preserved the
history and heritage of a property, while injecting a bit of funk into the fade.

It's sometimes hard to believe that this house only came back to life in the
past few years, because it feels so loved and lived-in. Entering it for the first

LEFT A view of the attic suite, which is pared back and minimal but, nevertheless, charming in its simplicity. An antique tapestry chair stands outside the double bedroom.

RIGHT Floorboards are painted white throughout this floor, making it light and airy. A bright yellow door brings a flash of colour to the bathroom.

time through the flagstone hallway, past the rows of Wellington boots and into the warm kitchen with its views of the courtyard, you have to remind yourself that this isn't a family home and that you haven't just strolled into the house of a friend (though I have to admit that sadly I don't know anyone with an art collection like this one!). Yes, it's full of awe inspiring art, but I can assure you, that once you've made a cup of tea and put your feet up, you'd feel right at home and that's quite an achievement. It's a perfect English farmhouse and yet it's also a commercial art venture. It's not so much Airbnb, more Artbnb and that's what makes it unique.

Bohemian Faded Glamour

LEFT Sera Hersham-Loftus' signature 'House Gowns' feature throughout the apartment she refers to as the 'Little Venice Rooms'. These beautiful curtains – made from recycled pieces of lace, crochet, muslin and velvet, which are then hand dyed – serve as room dividers, wall hangings and window dressings. On the walls are paintings she inherited from her father, art dealer Leslie Hersham.

OVERLEAF Wooden floorboards from Amsterdam are used in the main living space and throughout the apartment. 'You do get the odd splinter,' she laughs, 'but I would never have them treated because I love the look of them.' Behind her Emmanuelle peacock chair hang rope sculptures by the Canadian artist Annie Legault, one of the many artists and designers Sera supports, showing their work in the apartment which doubles as her atelier.

Describing the style of the designer Sera Hersham-Loftus is not an easy task, and even if I'd devoted the whole of this book to her, I'd still be struggling! Is it Bohemian…? Yes (though she hates that word). Is it elegant…? Of course. Romantic…? Very much so. Shabby chic…? In places, though I'd argue that it can be better described as sophisticated glamour. It's sumptuous, seductive, exotic and highly unique.

If I had to sum up Sera's style in a word, then I would opt for 'theatre', because when you enter her London apartment for the first time it's like walking onto a stage, which isn't that surprising when you consider that she began her career working on opera sets.

The reason why it's so hard to define Sera's style is that it's constantly evolving, ever-changing and she doesn't go by the rules. To give you an example of this, Sera doesn't measure up – doing everything by eye – and she completely 'hates' walls, which I find quite amusing given that she spends her life decorating the houses of the rich and famous. 'I just find them really boring and constrictive,' she says, smiling. 'They can just be so bland.' Her Little Venice apartment is a testament to this. Rather than being laid out in a succession of readily distinguishable rooms that we are all familiar with, it's more a giant living space. It's part boudoir, part salon, part atelier… and that's what makes it so thrilling.

Sera bought the property more than two decades ago from a DJ friend and quickly set about putting her own stamp on it. Rooms were knocked through to create a central living space. Carpets were ripped out and replaced with untreated floorboards imported by truck from Amsterdam – as was an entire panelled room so she could line her 'bland' walls. The chimneypiece above the French stone fireplace was stripped of its

LEFT An antique armchair in worn and torn amethyst silk stands in front of one of the vast pot plants that Sera has filled her house with. These giant palms and ferns are her pride and joy: she wanted to give the apartment the feeling of an indoor garden. At night, they are lit with amber light bulbs to create the ambience of a midnight garden. Vintage trunks stacked next to the chair serve as a table and provide storage.

RIGHT Sera's hand-drawn designs for her interiors projects on her antique dining room table. Flowers are in abundance in her apartment, adding to the romantic feeling of the property.

plaster to expose bare brick; ceilings were painted black, as was the kitchen. Against this backdrop she placed day-beds and antique furniture from past decades, which she wasn't afraid to mix up, and hung paintings inherited from her father, who was the renowned art dealer Leslie Hersham. She ripped out the light fittings, lighting the apartment with amber bulbs hidden within her jungle of vast potted plants; placed a retro Emmanuelle wicker chair by the fire; and hung a giant disco ball – which she likes to think came from Studio 54 – above her elegant salon seating area. 'It's a bit Anita Pallenberg, a bit Vermeer,' she says. 'I like to think that in a parallel universe

LEFT House gowns serve
as room dividers between
the central living space and
the bedroom. The walls are
covered in panels which she
acquired from an apartment in
Amsterdam, where she also
found her floorboards.

OVERLEAF Sera's bespoke
kitchen was designed to look
like a lacquered chest. The
black tiles were custom-made.
'I'm a great believer in
craftsmanship,' she says, 'it's
important that we respect that
art and support people with
those skills.' The 1970s kitchen
chairs have been reupholstered
in quilted silver leather. On the
back wall of the kitchen, Sera
has collated photographs of
family and friends. 'I much
prefer showing them like that
than having them in frames.'

had they shacked up together, this would be the apartment they would have
put together!'

Separating the living space from her bedroom, bathroom, dressing room,
working and eating areas are the most beautiful panels of fabric. These are
her signature 'House Gowns,' from her label Sera and Sestra. Handmade
muslin curtains, appliquéd with vintage lace and hand dyed, are designed to
be hung over windows and walls, used to separate spaces and replace
doors. These exquisite textiles, which have become hugely covetable, not
only give the apartment a romantic feel but also allow the space to be a

LEFT A vast day-bed, dressed with cushions of velvet and silk in shell-like shapes from Sera's collection, is not just inviting, but gives the room a feeling of old-school Hollywood glamour.

RIGHT With its panelled walls, beautifully dressed floor-to-ceiling windows and antique mirrors, Sera's salon is the height of elegance. With buttons, hessian and horsehair exposed, Sera refers to the armchairs in the centre as her 'naked' chairs. A giant disco ball hangs from the black-painted ceiling. 'Unfortunately it doesn't spin,' she explains, 'I'd love it to turn, but it's so heavy I think the ceiling might come crashing down!'

OVERLEAF A view of Sera's dressing room, with antique French shutters – adorned with her collection of ballet shoes – as an alternative to wardrobe doors. The lampshade atop the lamp on the right of the room is one of her own designs.

moveable feast. In the winter, she suspends them from her bedroom ceiling over a vast mattress on the floor to create a flowing makeshift four-poster bed. In the summer, she moves them into the central living space so she can sleep on a large day-bed and enjoy the evening breeze. 'What I love about them is that they don't allow a space to ever really be defined.'

The one room that is defined – apart from her sumptuous bathroom – is the kitchen. Here she commissioned a craftsman to create what I can only describe as possibly the most glamorous range of kitchen units I have ever seen, in black lacquer and brass. The 1970s kitchen chairs were another of

LEFT House gowns separate the dressing room from the bathroom, which is decorated with handmade black and white chevron tiles. A haberdasher's chest provides clever storage. The window has been dressed with vintage lace.

RIGHT A look into Sera's wonderfully romantic bedroom. House gowns are used here to create a four-poster look around her giant mattress. On winter nights, she lights the fire in the original stone fireplace.

her finds, which she had reupholstered in silver leather. If Barbarella were to own a pair of kitchen chairs, then I imagine these would be hers.

As a designer who, when not dressing the houses of celebrities, is called upon to put clothes on their backs when heading to an awards ceremony, wedding, or festival, Sera loves her clothes. This is a woman who was doing vintage long before it became fashionable – when it used to be called 'second hand' – and her dressing room does not disappoint. Her collection of vintage clothes and shoes is cleverly hidden away by authentic, antique French window shutters, while some are draped decoratively on the walls.

LEFT AND RIGHT When she isn't dressing the houses of the rich and famous, Sera is often called upon to act as their stylist, and her collection of vintage clothes is to die for. As someone who was wearing and collecting vintage long before the rest of us, she has some exquisite pieces which she loves to display throughout her apartment.

Her love of all things bright and beautiful explains her passion for flora and fauna. Not a table in the apartment is without a vintage vase or vessel filled with wild blooms. 'As for the plants – they bring me huge joy, I couldn't live without them. They bring a bit of the outside in and put a smile on my face.'

When I first brought my youngest daughter Betty to Sera's apartment, she was breathless with excitement. 'Why can't we live like this?' she asked wide-eyed. Seeing the apartment through her eyes, I had to agree, for this is every little girl's (and big girl's – like me) dream home – a giant, wafty, dressing-up box that we'd all like to immerse ourselves in, even for a night.

Relaxed Faded Glamour

LEFT To their delight, the
Richards inherited the beautiful
William Morris wallpapers from
the previous owners. Though
slightly faded with time, the
timeless pattern suits the
proportions of the property and
provides the perfect backdrop
for their art and furniture.
Hanging above the marble
fireplace is a mirror in a frame
made from elm. A drinks
cabinet in a bright, distressed
blue was a flea market find.

OVERLEAF In the living
room, comfort is key and styles
are mixed. A large, classic
George Smith armchair faces
one in leather with a wooden
frame. Blankets, wool cushions
and large vintage rugs covering
the wooden floor add warmth
to the room. Contemporary
art mixes with older pieces
and portraits throughout
the downstairs.

A trip to the wonderful home of Simon and Alicia Richards is worth it for the views alone. Perched high upon a hill, on a bright day from the bay window in their dining room you can see Somerset – with its rolling hills and vales – in its full splendid glory. But there is another reason why I adore this house, and it's because of the way that its owners have utilised the space and breathed character and life into this former Victorian vicarage.

Built in 1850, the house benefits from all the features of that period – generously proportioned rooms, high ceilings, vast fireplaces, floor-to-ceiling windows, cornicing and shutter work – which was exactly what the Richards were dreaming of when they bought the property twenty years ago, because this house wasn't going to just be a weekend bolthole for the cinematographer and his wife, a successful advertising producer, but a family home where they would raise their children.

Location was obviously key to the Richards so they'd be near to the children's schools, as was space, being a family of five. As such, they were prepared to take on a wreck when they began their house hunt. What they weren't expecting when they first walked across the threshold of the vicarage was to find a house that had been lovingly restored by its previous owners. Rooms they had imagined they would need to paint were lined with beautiful William Morris wallpapers and the historic paintwork round the windows and shutters, though peeling in places, only had to be retouched. It already had that shabby chic feel and that was before they even moved a stick of their stunning furniture in – pieces they had been collecting for years. A classic George Smith sofa is mixed with a 1950s green leather chair in the living room. Objects, artifacts and quirky religious candles, all collected on the couple's travels, adorn every surface. Each painting has a story to tell.

LEFT The etched-glass wooden-framed sliding door – which Simon designed himself using old door frames he had in storage – separates the eating area from the family's den. Two large coolie shades hang over the table.

RIGHT A sumptuous green scalloped leather chair from the 1950s was bought by the couple over twenty years ago in London's Notting Hill.

OVERLEAF, LEFT Dotted around the house are curios and objects collected on their extensive travels around the world. Vases, pots, gem-coloured glass candlesticks and quirky religious veladoras and votives that were found on trips to Mexico and California.

OVERLEAF, RIGHT An upright piano with a stool that has been filled with sheet music handed down through generations of the family.

Central to the house is the dining room, where at their 15-foot long antique French farmhouse table the couple regularly entertain hordes of family and friends. They have sectioned off the eating area from the children's den with clever use of sliding doors. Simon had them in storage before the couple even found the house. 'I have a thing about doors – I seem to collect them,' he laughs. 'I hadn't a clue what I was going to do with them, and when we moved here it just made sense because they act like a screen.' By inserting etched glass into the doorframes they could create privacy without losing light when the doors were closed,

LEFT The bay window in the dining room, with its magnificent views of the Somerset countryside below. The dining-room chairs and the four-foot wrought iron cross by the window came from Succession in Westbourne Grove, London. The chandelier hanging above the table has been given a rainbow of old, colourful shades.

and by having them be sliding, rather than hinged, they haven't lost any space.

The chandelier above the dining-room table was a gift from a director friend of the couple. Slightly falling apart and in need of a little TLC, Simon set about restoring it, and to give it an extra twist added mismatched vintage lampshades he found along the way. 'I'm fond of projects like that,' he confesses. 'And it does give off a lovely light at night from the different coloured shades and the crystals. Plus, it's a bit of a talking point.' There are many talking points dotted around the Richards' house, that's for sure. Not least the view, which I'd say has to be one of the best in the whole of the county.

RIGHT What I love about this vicarage is its character and Alicia and Simon have celebrated that while injecting their own personality into the property. It's in the mix of furniture, art and religious paraphernalia dotted round the house. In fact, I was so inspired by the Richards' quirky style that one of the first things I did when I moved into my own house was to install a china rabbit into this alcove as a witty homage to them.

Resources & Suppliers

Pearl Lowe

www.pearllowe.co.uk
Instagram: @pearllowe
pinterest.com/pearllowedesign

Artist credits

Pages 156–157: Phyllida Barlow,
untitled: streetleaningobjects, 2011
© Phyllida Barlow
Courtesy of Phyllida Barlow and
Hauser & Wirth

Pages 163–163: Phyllida Barlow,
untitled, 2002
© Phyllida Barlow
Courtesy of Phyllida Barlow and
Hauser & Wirth

Page 165: Phyllida Barlow, untitled:
greenstacksandtubes, 2, 2012
© Phyllida Barlow
Courtesy of Phyllida Barlow and
Hauser & Wirth

Page 167: Phyllida Barlow, untitled,
2002
© Phyllida Barlow
Courtesy of Phyllida Barlow and
Hauser & Wirth

Page 170: Phyllida Barlow, untitled
1999
© Phyllida Barlow
Courtesy of Phyllida Barlow and
Hauser & Wirth

Page 172: Rita Ackermann,
Fire by Days XXXIX
© Rita Ackermann
Courtesy of Rita Ackermann
and Hauser & Wirth

Vintage and antiques

Alfies Antique Market
alfiesantiques.com; 0207 723 6066

Anne Fowler
annefowlertetbury.co.uk;
01666 504043

Baileys Home
baileyshome.com; 01989 561931

B & T Antiques
bntantiques.co.uk; 0207 229 7001

Betty & Violet
bettyandviolet.com; 01386 859126

Chloe Antiques
chloeantiques.co.uk; 07977 127862

Cloth House
clothhouse.com; 0207 437 5155

Crowman Antiques
01380 725548

Dairy House Antiques
dairyhouseantiques.co.uk;
01747 853317

Daisy Roots Vintage
daisyrootsvintage.co.uk;
01409 211465

Decorative Collective
decorativecollective.com

Decorative Country Living
decorativecountryliving.com;
01400 273632

Dig Haüshizzle
dig-haushizzle.co.uk; 07789 145175

Drew Pritchard Antiques
drewpritchard.co.uk; 01492 580890

Eversley Barn Antiques
eversleybarnantiques.co.uk;
0118 932 8518

French General Trading
frenchgeneraltrading.co.uk;
01373 466155

Gingerlily
gingerlily.co.uk; 0208 877 9905

**Grace Decorative Interiors
& Clothing**
gracedecorative.co.uk;
01985 213208

Haus
haus-interiors.co.uk; 01428 653336

Jasper Jacks
jasperjacks.com; 07508 527787

Kilver Court
kilvercourt.com; 01749 340422

La Belle Brocante, Wells
01749 672164

La Belle Étoffe
labelleetoffe.co.uk; 07973 829553

La Belle Maison
jeffinie-labellemaison.blogspot.co.uk;
07903 173045

Les Couilles du Chien
lescouillesduchien.com;
020 8968 0099

Llewelyn & Co
llewelynandcompany.com;
01497 821880

Original House
original-house.co.uk; 07909 581411

Pimpernel & Partners
pimpernelandpartners.co.uk;
07929 340227

Poppy Greens Home
poppygreens.co.uk; 01749 678912

Phoenix
phoenixongolborne.co.uk;
0208 964 8123

RE
re-foundobjects.com; 01434 634567

Retrouvius
retrouvius.com; 020 8960 6060

Rockett St George
rockettstgeorge.co.uk; 01444 253391

Ruby Lane
rubylane.com

Samaya Ling Vintage
samayalingvintage.com;
07877 057082

Sera Hersham-Loftus
seraoflondon.com; 07977 534115

**Susannah Decorative Antiques and
Textiles**
cloudsandangels.com; 01225 445069

The Cross
thecrossshop.co.uk; 020 7727 6760

The Fig Store
01666 505716

The French Depot
thefrenchdepot.com; 01424 423703

The Old Albion
theoldalbion.com; 07879 051362

Interiors

Anthropologie
www.anthropologie.eu
www.anthropologie.com

Agapanthus Interiors
agapanthusinteriors.com;
0161 429 9710

Arbon Interiors
arbon-interiors.mysupadupa.com

Berry Red
berryred.co.uk; 01432 265094

Bert & May
bertandmay.com; 0203 744 0776

Beyond France
beyondfrance.co.uk; 07710 148915

Cabbages & Roses
cabbagesandroses.com;
0207 352 7333

Cath Kidston
cathkidston.com

Cox & Cox
coxandcox.co.uk; 0330 333 2123

deVOL Kitchens
devolkitchens.co.uk; 0203 879 7900

Dilliway & Dilliway
dilliway.co.uk; 01458 833463

Domestic Science
domscihome.wordpress.com

eBay
ebay.com

Etsy
etsy.com

Emily Rose Vintage
emilyrosevintage.co.uk

Fired Earth
firedearth.com; 01295 812088

Graham & Green
grahamandgreen.co.uk;
01225 418200

IKEA
ikea.com

Magnolia Pearl
magnoliapearl.com;
001 830 990 9600

Martha Stewart
marthastewart.com

Not on the High Street
notonthehighstreet.com;
0203 318 5115

Odd Limited
www.oddlimited.com; 01993 830674

Pedlars
pedlars.co.uk; 0207 727 7799

Plain English
plainenglishdesign.co.uk;
0207 486 2674

Rachel Ashwell
shabbychic.com

Soho Home
sohohome.com

Summerill & Bishop
summerillandbishop.com;
0207 221 4566

The French House
thefrenchhouse.net; 0207 859 4939

Welbeck Tiles
welbeck.com; 01736 762000

Wallpaper, textiles, paint and accessories

Anna French
annafrench.co.uk; 0207 737 6555/ 001
800 223 0704

Annie Sloan
anniesloan.com; 01865 770061

Carey Lind Design
careylinddesign.com

Celia Birtwell
celiabirtwell.com

Cole & Son
cole-and-son.com; 0208 442 8844

Denholme Velvets
denholme-velvets.co.uk;
01274 832185

Diptyque
diptyqueparis.com

East London Parasol Company
eastlondonparasols.com

Elanbach
elanbach.com; 01543 410550

Farrow & Ball
farrow-ball.com; 01202 876141

GF Smith
gfsmith.com; 0207 394 4660

Goutal
goutalparis.com

House of Hackney
houseofhackney.com; 020 7739 3273

ibbi
ibbidirect.co.uk; 01434 409085

James Hare
james-hare.com; 01132 431204

Jimmy Cricket
jimmycricket.com.au

John Lewis
johnlewis.com

Kate Forman
kateforman.co.uk; 01962 732244

The Linen Works
thelinenworks.com; 0203 744 1020

Little Greene
littlegreene.com; 0845 880 5855

Miss Print
missprint.co.uk; 01277 350581

Morton, Young & Borland Textiles
mybtextiles.com; 01560 321210

Nicholas Herbert
nicholasherbert.com; 0207 376 5596

Osborne & Little
osborneandlittle.com

Parna
parna.co.uk; 07906 420685

Penny Morrison
pennymorrison.com; 0207 384 2975

Pongees
pongees.co.uk; 0207 739 9130

Ralph Lauren
ralphlaurenhome.com

Robert Kime
robertkime.com; 0207 831 6066

Roger Oates Design
rogeroates.com; 01531 632718

Rothschild & Bickers
rothschildbickers.com;
0207 359 5817

Rosie's Vintage Wallpaper
rosiesvintagewallpaper.com;
001 618 231 2196

Select Wallpaper
selectwallpaper.co.uk; 01382 477000

Sister Parish
sisterparishdesign.com

Style Library
stylelibrary.com; 0203 4575 862

V V Rouleaux
vvrouleaux.com; 0207 224 5179

Wallpaper Direct
wallpaperdirect.com

Wendy Morrison
wendymorrisondesign.com;
07743 943486

Clothes and accessories

Bill Amberg
billamberg.com; 0208 960 2000

Lark Vintage
larkvintage.co.uk

Solange Azagury-Partridge
solange.co.uk; 0207 792 0197

Temperley London
temperleylondon.com;
0207 313 4756

Vintage china and flowers

Article
articlebath.com; 01225 460189

Bramble & Wild
brambleandwild.com; 01373 473788

Daisy Valentine Flowers
daisyvalentine.com; 01963 351414

Elsie Florence
elsieflorence.co.uk; 01963 32752

Everything Stops for Tea
everythingstopsfortea.com;
01629 821822

Passion Flowers
flowersbypassion.com;
01225 859994

Scarlet & Violet
www.scarletandviolet.com;
0208 969 9446

Susie Bell
beyondbeleaf.co.uk

The Real Flower Company
realflowers.co.uk; 01730 818300

White Row Florist
whiterowflorist.co.uk; 01373 830024

Fleamarkets

For fairs and fleamarkets, check
the internet or local newspapers
for events and venues. Here are
some general websites you can try:

antiqueweb.co.uk

antiques-atlas.com

discovervintage.co.uk
07880 910361

iacf.co.uk
(International Antiques and
Collector's Fairs); 01636 702326

judysvintagefair.co.uk

ukvintagefairs.com

Reclamation

Antique Bathrooms of Ivybridge
antiquebaths.com; 01752 698250

Frome Reclamation
fromerec.co.uk; 01373 463919

Glastonbury Reclamation
glastonburyreclamation.co.uk;
01458 831122

UKAA Ltd
ukaa.com; 01543 222923

Wells Reclamation
wellsreclamation.com; 01749 677087

Index

Page numbers in *italics* refer to illustrations

Acknowledgments

I'd like to thank my long-suffering husband Danny – without his patience and good nature I never would have been allowed to experiment in our houses in the way that I have. I'd also like to thank my four wonderful children: Daisy, Alfie, Frankie and Betty, for putting up with our endless house moves and for being a constant source of inspiration to me. Thanks to my Mum, without her guidance and good taste this book would never have happened. Thank you to the lovely Anita, who has helped keep our house and family together. Thank you to my bestie Zoe, for not only being there for me through thick and thin, but also for listening to me drone on about interiors for the last God knows how many years!

Thank you so much to my wonderful friend Rachel Ashwell who came up with the idea for this book. Without her support, help and vision, I could never have created it – her art direction and experience were invaluable. Thank you, of course, to Amy Neunsinger for the beautiful images and for making the whole process so much fun, to Devon for all her technical support, to Belle for her organisation and style, and to the incredible homeowners, of course, for allowing us into their fabulous homes. Thank you to CICO Books for allowing me the freedom to create this book, in particular Geoff Borin for his lovely design, Natasha Garnett for her ability to capture my voice so perfectly, Anna Galkina for her careful editing, Sally Powell for overseeing the design and especially Cindy Richards for commissioning this book. We got there in the end!